THE ANGLICAN ROSARY AND THE LECTIONARY

THE REVISED COMMON LECTIONARY

RICK MORLEY

AN INTRODUCTION

Scripture can—and should!—be studied. We should "read, mark, learn, and inwardly digest" it.

Scripture can—and should!—be read during worship. And, scripture should be the fertile soil from which a sermon or homily springs forth.

The ancient liturgy of the church—preserved in most liturgical churches—is set up so that large portions of the scriptures are read from, and then everything that follows the readings becomes a response to them: sermon, creed, prayers, confession, the passing of the peace, and Eucharist. That then becomes a model for how Christians live our whole lives: everything we do is a response to what God has shared with us in the pages of the Bible.

Scripture can—and should!—also be prayed. Large portions of the scriptures themselves are indeed prayers. The Book of Psalms is a massive collection of prayers. Some are prayers of praise, some are prayers of contrition, some are raw prayers prayed in moments of great grief and loss, and some are prayers that were designed for whole communities to pray together when they gathered for a festival or other grand occasion.

Our ancient forebears often prayed with scripture. Lectio Divina—an ancient method of praying with the scriptures—has received a huge comeback in recent years, and has inspired "Dwelling in the Word" as a way for a group of people to pray the scriptures together. Ignatius of Loyola taught us how to use our imaginations to enter into the stories of scripture and locate ourselves right there—looking for new insights, and for what God is trying to tell us personally, as we walk along the Sea of Galilee with Jesus, as we ascend the mountain with Moses, and as we sit down at the Last Supper amongst the disciples.

The rosary is another ancient Christian tool for praying with scripture. The traditional rosary uses the Lord's Prayer, which is lifted right out of the pages of the Gospels. And, it uses the Hail Mary, which begins with two scripture citations from the Gospel of Luke. The traditional rosary also invites the person praying it to reflect and meditate on various aspects of the life of Jesus—called "mysteries"—while praying through the set prayers.

For centuries, Christians have prayed the rosary, and in so doing, each time, we have been praying with scripture.

A few decades ago, Anglican Christians took the traditional rosary and put a new spin on it creating the

"Anglican Rosary." Instead of five sections of ten beads, there are four sections of seven beads. Seven, of course, refers neatly to the days of creation, and with four sections the whole thing has a cross-like shape to it. There are a total of thirty-three beads on the rosary, which corresponds to the years of the life of Jesus of Nazareth.

This new form of rosary was, in part, inspired by a desire to give a beaded prayer resource to Christians who might be less comfortable directing so many prayers to Mary. However, these two rosaries don't have to be exclusive of each other. They are different tools of prayer that do different things—and you could use either, or both.

For me, the Anglican rosary offers a unique opportunity to pray with scripture—specifically the scriptures of the Sunday lectionary. Because the Anglican rosary is so much newer than its more ancient counterpart, the prayers assigned to the beads are less authoritative, which means that you can mold the Anglican rosary to your own use, day-by-day and week-by-week.

In this little book you'll find Anglican rosary prayers for each week of Year A, using the readings from the Revised Common Lectionary and two selections from The Book of Common Prayer (US, 1979). Each week's prayers begin with the seasonal Antiphon from Morning Prayer, and they end with the Collect of the Day.

I could imagine two ways of using this resource. The first is that on the particular Sunday, you go to church, hear the lessons, and then use those lessons as the basis for your prayers with the rosary through the week. After worshipping with these texts, you then graft them into your heart.

The second way is that on Monday you begin using the rosary to pray through the lessons for the upcoming Sunday, so that when you go to worship you have already been grafting the words of these lessons in your heart for a whole week.

As a priest and preacher, this is my preferred method. Of course through the week I'm studying the lessons in preparation for my homily, but with the rosary I am also praying with the lessons. It's been an exceedingly helpful practice for me, both personally and vocationally.

A QUICK USER GUIDE

An Anglican Rosary has a CROSS (usually different from traditional rosaries which have a crucifix) which connects directly to an INVITATORY bead. Then on the loop there are four CRUCIFORM beads which are separated by four sets of seven WEEK beads.

You can pray the CROSS, the INVITATORY bead, and then once around the loop, or you could choose to go three times around the loop.

However many times you go around, you can close your time with some personal prayers and the Lord's Prayer, the General Thanksgiving, the Grace, and/or the Collect for the Day.

When praying, you'll probably need the booklet for the prayers on the INVITATORY bead, as they tend to be a little longer, and are only prayed once. But, as you pray through the week, you should consider finding ways to put the book down. You should be able to memorize the WEEK bead prayer pretty quickly. Then, eventually, the CRUCIFORM bead prayer should find its way to being memorized. This will free you to close your eyes, and take your attention away from the words themselves, and direct that attention to where God wants it to be.

Allow the words to become conduits to God's Presence, God's Voice, and God's Bidding. God may use these words in prayer to speak deeper things than the words themselves.

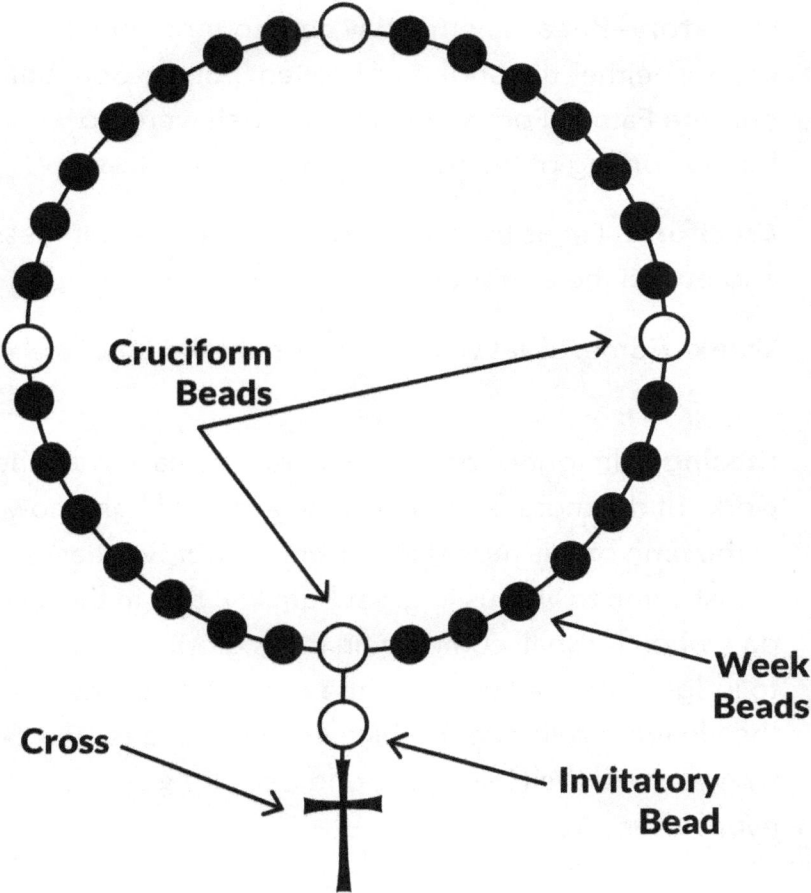

Cross–Our King and Savior now draws near: Come, let us adore him. *(BCP)*

Invitatory–But about that day and hour no one knows, neither the angels of heaven, nor the Son, but only the Father. For as the days of Noah were, so will be the coming of the Son of Man. *(Matthew 24:36)*

Cruciform–Let us then lay aside the works of darkness and put on the armor of light. *(Romans 13:12)*

Week–Come, us let walk in the light of the Lord! *(Isaiah 2:5)*

Closing–Almighty God, give us grace to cast away the works of darkness, and put on the armor of light, now in the time of this mortal life in which your Son Jesus Christ came to visit us in great humility; that in the last day, when he shall come again in his glorious majesty to judge both the living and the dead, we may rise to the life immortal; through him who lives and reigns with you and the Holy Spirit, one God, now and for ever. Amen. *(BCP)*

Cross—Our King and Savior now draws near: Come, let us adore him. *(BCP)*

Invitatory—The root of Jesse shall come, the one who rises to rule the Gentiles; in him the Gentiles shall hope." *(Romans 15:12)*

Cruciform—The voice of one crying out in the wilderness: 'Prepare the way of the Lord, make his paths straight.' *(Matthew 3:3)*

Week—A shoot shall come out from the stump of Jesse, and a branch shall grow out of his roots. *(Isaiah 11:1)*

Closing—Merciful God, who sent your messengers the prophets to preach repentance and prepare the way for our salvation: Give us grace to heed their warnings and forsake our sins, that we may greet with joy the coming of Jesus Christ our Redeemer; who lives and reigns with you and the Holy Spirit, one God, now and for ever. Amen. *(BCP)*

Cross—Our King and Savior now draws near: Come, let us adore him. *(BCP)*

Invitatory—The wilderness and the dry land shall be glad, the desert shall rejoice and blossom; like the crocus it shall blossom abundantly, and rejoice with joy and singing. *(Isaiah 35:1)*

Cruciform—My soul proclaims the greatness of the Lord, my spirit rejoices in God my Savior. *(Luke 1:46)*

Week—Be patient, therefore, beloved, until the coming of the Lord. *(James 5:7)*

Closing—Stir up your power, O Lord, and with great might come among us; and, because we are sorely hindered by our sins, let your bountiful grace and mercy speedily help and deliver us; through Jesus Christ our Lord, to whom, with you and the Holy Spirit, be honor and glory, now and for ever. Amen. *(BCP)*

THE FOURTH SUNDAY OF ADVENT

Cross—Our King and Savior now draws near: Come, let us adore him. *(BCP)*

Invitatory—[*For we are*] set apart for the gospel of God, which he promised beforehand through his prophets in the holy scriptures, the gospel concerning his Son, who was descended from David according to the flesh and was declared to be Son of God. *(Romans 1:1-4)*

Cruciform—Restore us, O God of hosts; show the light of your countenance, and we shall be saved. *(Psalm 80:18)*

Week—Look, the virgin shall conceive and bear a son, and they shall name him Emmanuel. *(Matthew 1:23)*

Closing—Purify our conscience, Almighty God, by your daily visitation, that your Son Jesus Christ, at his coming, may find in us a mansion prepared for himself; who lives and reigns with you, in the unity of the Holy Spirit, one God, now and for ever. Amen. *(BCP)*

Cross–Alleluia. To us a child is born; O come, let us adore him. Alleluia. *(BCP)*

Invitatory–In the beginning was the Word, and the Word was with God, and the Word was God. He was in the beginning with God. All things came into being through him, and without him not one thing came into being. *(John 1:1-3)*

Cruciform–And the Word became flesh and lived among us, and we have seen his glory, the glory as of a father's only son, full of grace and truth. *(John 1:14)*

Week–When the fullness of time had come, God sent his Son, born of a woman. *(Galatians 4:4)*

Closing–Almighty God, you have poured upon us the new light of your incarnate Word: Grant that this light, enkindled in our hearts, may shine forth in our lives; through Jesus Christ our Lord, who lives and reigns with you, in the unity of the Holy Spirit, one God, now and for ever. Amen. *(BCP)*

THE SECOND SUNDAY AFTER CHRISTMAS

Cross—Alleluia. To us a child is born; O come, let us adore him. Alleluia. *(BCP)*

Invitatory—After the wise men had left, an angel of the Lord appeared to Joseph in a dream and said, "Get up, take the child and his mother, and flee to Egypt." *(Matthew 2:13)*

Cruciform—Sing aloud with gladness for Jacob, and raise shouts for the chief of the nations. *(Jeremiah 31:7)*

Week—He destined us for adoption as his children through Jesus Christ. *(Ephesians 1:5)*

Closing—O God, who wonderfully created, and yet more wonderfully restored, the dignity of human nature: Grant that we may share the divine life of him who humbled himself to share our humanity, your Son Jesus Christ; who lives and reigns with you, in the unity of the Holy Spirit, one God, for ever and ever. Amen. *(BCP)*

THE FIRST SUNDAY AFTER THE EPIPHANY

Cross–The Lord has shown forth his glory: Come let us adore him. *(BCP)*

Invitatory–When Jesus had been baptized, just as he came up from the water, suddenly the heavens were opened to him. *(Matthew 3:16)*

Cruciform–He saw the Spirit of God descending like a dove and alighting on him. *(Matthew 3:16)*

Week–A voice from heaven said, "This is my Son, the Beloved, with whom I am well pleased." *(Matthew 3:17)*

Closing–Father in heaven, who at the baptism of Jesus in the River Jordan proclaimed him your beloved Son and anointed him with the Holy Spirit: Grant that all who are baptized into his Name may keep the covenant they have made, and boldly confess him as Lord and Savior; who with you and the Holy Spirit lives and reigns, one God, in glory everlasting. Amen. *(BCP)*

THE SECOND SUNDAY AFTER THE EPIPHANY

Cross–The Lord has shown forth his glory: Come let us adore him. *(BCP)*

Invitatory–Here is the Lamb of God who takes away the sin of the world. *(John 1:29)*

Cruciform–The Lord called me before I was born, while I was in my mother's womb he named me. *(Isaiah 49:1)*

Week–You are the Lord; let your love and your faithfulness keep me safe forever. *(Psalm 40:11)*

Closing–Almighty God, whose Son our Savior Jesus Christ is the light of the world: Grant that your people, illumined by your Word and Sacraments, may shine with the radiance of Christ's glory, that he may be known, worshiped, and obeyed to the ends of the earth; through Jesus Christ our Lord, who with you and the Holy Spirit lives and reigns, one God, now and for ever. Amen. *(BCP)*

THE THIRD SUNDAY AFTER THE EPIPHANY

Cross–The Lord has shown forth his glory: Come let us adore him. *(BCP)*

Invitatory–Jesus went throughout Galilee, teaching in their synagogues and proclaiming the good news of the kingdom and curing every disease and every sickness among the people. *(Matthew 4:23)*

Cruciform–For the message about the cross is foolishness to those who are perishing, but to us who are being saved it is the power of God. *(I Corinthians 1:18)*

Week–Repent for the kingdom of heaven has come near. *(Matthew 4:17)*

Closing–Give us grace, O Lord, to answer readily the call of our Savior Jesus Christ and proclaim to all people the Good News of his salvation, that we and the whole world may perceive the glory of his marvelous works; who lives and reigns with you and the Holy Spirit, one God, for ever and ever. Amen. *(BCP)*

THE FOURTH SUNDAY AFTER THE EPIPHANY

Cross–The Lord has shown forth his glory: Come let us adore him. *(BCP)*

Invitatory–When Jesus saw the crowds, he went up the mountain; and after he sat down, his disciples came to him. Then he began to speak. *(Matthew 5:1)*

Cruciform–The message about the cross is foolishness to those who are perishing, but to us who are being saved it is the power of God. *(I Corinthians 1:18)*

Week–Blessed are the poor in spirit, for theirs is the kingdom of heaven. *(Matthew 5:3)*

Closing–Almighty and everlasting God, you govern all things both in heaven and on earth: Mercifully hear the supplications of your people, and in our time grant us your peace; through Jesus Christ our Lord, who lives and reigns with you and the Holy Spirit, one God, for ever and ever. Amen. *(BCP)*

THE FIFTH SUNDAY AFTER THE EPIPHANY

Cross—The Lord has shown forth his glory: Come let us adore him. *(BCP)*

Invitatory—Jesus said, "You are the salt of the earth; but if salt has lost its taste, how can its saltiness be restored? *(Matthew 5:13)*

Cruciform—Now we have received not the spirit of the world, but the Spirit that is from God. *(I Corinthians 2:12)*

Week—You are the light of the world. A city built on a hill cannot be hid. *(Matthew 5:14)*

Closing—Set us free, O God, from the bondage of our sins, and give us the liberty of that abundant life which you have made known to us in your Son our Savior Jesus Christ; who lives and reigns with you, in the unity of the Holy Spirit, one God, now and for ever. Amen. *(BCP)*

THE SIXTH SUNDAY AFTER THE EPIPHANY

Cross–The Lord has shown forth his glory: Come let us adore him. *(BCP)*

Invitatory–Choose life so that you and your descendants may live, loving the Lord your God, obeying him, and holding fast to him. *(Deuteronomy 30:20)*

Cruciform–You laid down your commandments, that we should fully keep them. *(Psalm 199:4)*

Week–For we are God's servants, working together; you are God's field, God's building. *(I Corinthians 3:9)*

Closing–O God, the strength of all who put their trust in you: Mercifully accept our prayers; and because in our weakness we can do nothing good without you, give us the help of your grace, that in keeping your commandments we may please you both in will and deed; through Jesus Christ our Lord, who lives and reigns with you and the Holy Spirit, one God, for ever and ever. Amen. *(BCP)*

THE SEVENTH SUNDAY AFTER THE EPIPHANY

Cross–The Lord has shown forth his glory: Come let us adore him. *(BCP)*

Invitatory–But I say to you, Love your enemies and pray for those who persecute you, so that you may be children of your Father in heaven. *(Matthew 5:44-45)*

Cruciform–Do you not know that you are God's temple and that God's Spirit dwells in you? *(I Corinthians 3:16)*

Week–All belong to you, and you belong to Christ, and Christ belongs to God. *(I Corinthians 3:23)*

Closing–O Lord, you have taught us that without love whatever we do is worth nothing; Send your Holy Spirit and pour into our hearts your greatest gift, which is love, the true bond of peace and of all virtue, without which whoever lives is accounted dead before you. Grant this for the sake of your only Son Jesus Christ, who lives and reigns with you and the Holy Spirit, one God, now and for ever. Amen. *(BCP)*

THE EIGHTH SUNDAY AFTER THE EPIPHANY

Cross—The Lord has shown forth his glory: Come let us adore him. *(BCP)*

Invitatory—Therefore I tell you, do not worry about your life, what you will eat or what you will drink, or about your body, what you will wear. Is not life more than food, and the body more than clothing? *(Matthew 6:25)*

Cruciform—Look at the birds of the air; they neither sow nor reap nor gather into barns, and yet your heavenly Father feeds them. *(Matthew 6:26)*

Week—Strive for the kingdom of God and his righteousness, and all these things will be given to you as well. *(Matthew 6:33)*

Closing—Most loving Father, whose will it is for us to give thanks for all things, to fear nothing but the loss of you, and to cast all our care on you who care for us: Preserve us from faithless fears and worldly anxieties, that no clouds of this mortal life may hide from us the light of that love which is immortal, and which you have manifested to us in your Son Jesus Christ our Lord; who lives and reigns with you, in the unity of the Holy Spirit, one God, now and for ever. Amen. *(BCP)*

THE LAST SUNDAY AFTER THE EPIPHANY

Cross–The Lord has shown forth his glory: Come let us adore him. *(BCP)*

Invitatory–We did not follow cleverly devised myths when we made known to you the power and coming of our Lord Jesus Christ, but we had been eyewitnesses of his majesty. *(2 Peter 1:16)*

Cruciform–Jesus came and touched them, saying, "Get up and do not be afraid. *(Matthew 17:7)*

Week–This is my Son, the Beloved; with him I am well pleased; listen to him! *(Matthew 17:5)*

Closing–O God, who before the passion of your only-begotten Son revealed his glory upon the holy mountain: Grant to us that we, beholding by faith the light of his countenance, may be strengthened to bear our cross, and be changed into his likeness from glory to glory; through Jesus Christ our Lord, who lives and reigns with you and the Holy Spirit, one God, for ever and ever. Amen. *(BCP)*

Cross–The Lord is full of compassion and mercy: Come let us adore him. *(BCP)*

Invitatory–Just as one man's trespass led to condemnation for all, so one man's act of righteousness leads to justification and life for all. *(Romans 5:18)*

Cruciform–One does not live by bread alone, but by every word that comes from the mouth of God. *(Matthew 4:4)*

Week–Worship the Lord your God, and serve only him. *(Matthew 4:10)*

Closing–Almighty God, whose blessed Son was led by the Spirit to be tempted by Satan: Come quickly to help us who are assaulted by many temptations; and, as you know the weaknesses of each of us, let each one find you mighty to save; through Jesus Christ your Son our Lord, who lives and reigns with you and the Holy Spirit, one God, now and for ever. Amen. *(BCP)*

Cross—The Lord is full of compassion and mercy: Come let us adore him. *(BCP)*

Invitatory—I lift up my eyes to the hills; from where is my help to come? My help comes from the Lord, the maker of heaven and earth. *(Psalm 121:1)*

Cruciform—For God so loved the world that he gave his only Son, so that everyone who believes in him may not perish but may have eternal life. *(John 3:16)*

Week— I will bless you, and make your name great, so that you will be a blessing. *(Genesis 12:2)*

Closing—O God, whose glory it is always to have mercy: Be gracious to all who have gone astray from your ways, and bring them again with penitent hearts and steadfast faith to embrace and hold fast the unchangeable truth of your Word, Jesus Christ your Son; who with you and the Holy Spirit lives and reigns, one God, for ever and ever. Amen. *(BCP)*

Cross—The Lord is full of compassion and mercy: Come let us adore him. *(BCP)*

Invitatory—Jesus answered her, "If you knew the gift of God, and who it is that is saying to you, 'Give me a drink,' you would have asked him, and he would have given you living water." *(John 4:10)*

Cruciform—Since we are justified by faith, we have peace with God through our Lord Jesus Christ. *(Romans 5:1)*

Week—Is the Lord among us or not? *(Exodus 17:7)*

Closing—Almighty God, you know that we have no power in ourselves to help ourselves: Keep us both outwardly in our bodies and inwardly in our souls, that we may be defended from all adversities which may happen to the body, and from all evil thoughts which may assault and hurt the soul; through Jesus Christ our Lord, who lives and reigns with you and the Holy Spirit, one God, for ever and ever. Amen. *(BCP)*

Cross–The Lord is full of compassion and mercy: Come let us adore him. *(BCP)*

Invitatory–Jesus said, "I came into this world for judgment so that those who do not see may see, and those who do see may become blind." *(John 9:39)*

Cruciform–Once you were darkness, but now in the Lord you are light. Live as children of light. *(Ephesians 5:8)*

Week–Sleeper, awake! Rise from the dead, and Christ will shine on you. *(Ephesians 5:14)*

Closing–Gracious Father, whose blessed Son Jesus Christ came down from heaven to be the true bread which gives life to the world: Evermore give us this bread, that he may live in us, and we in him; who lives and reigns with you and the Holy Spirit, one God, now and for ever. Amen. *(BCP)*

Cross–The Lord is full of compassion and mercy: Come let us adore him. *(BCP)*

Invitatory–Out of the depths have I called to you, O Lord; Lord, hear my voice. let your ears consider well the voice of my supplication. *(Psalm 130:1)*

Cruciform– The dead man came out, his hands and feet bound with strips of cloth, and his face wrapped in a cloth. Jesus said to them, "Unbind him, and let him go." *(John 11:34)*

Week– He said to me, "Mortal, can these bones live?" I answered, "O Lord God, you know." *(Ezekiel 37:3)*

Closing–Almighty God, you alone can bring into order the unruly wills and affections of sinners: Grant your people grace to love what you command and desire what you promise; that, among the swift and varied changes of the world, our hearts may surely there be fixed where true joys are to be found; through Jesus Christ our Lord, who lives and reigns with you and the Holy Spirit, one God, now and for ever. Amen. *(BCP)*

THE SUNDAY OF THE PASSION

Cross—The Lord is full of compassion and mercy: Come let us adore him. *(BCP)*

Invitatory—Hosanna to the Son of David! Blessed is the one who comes in the name of the Lord! Hosanna in the highest heaven! *(Matthew 21:9)*

Cruciform—And about three o'clock Jesus cried with a loud voice, "My God, my God, why have you forsaken me?" *(Matthew 27:46)*

Week—Let the same mind be in you that was in Christ Jesus. *(Philippians 2:5)*

Closing—Almighty and everliving God, in your tender love for the human race you sent your Son our Savior Jesus Christ to take upon him our nature, and to suffer death upon the cross, giving us the example of his great humility: Mercifully grant that we may walk in the way of his suffering, and also share in his resurrection; through Jesus Christ our Lord, who lives and reigns with you and the Holy Spirit, one God, for ever and ever. Amen. *(BCP)*

Cross–Alleluia. The Lord is risen indeed: Come, let us adore him. Alleluia. *(BCP)*

Invitatory–They put him to death by hanging him on a tree; but God raised him on the third day and allowed him to appear, not to all the people but to us who were chosen by God as witnesses, and who ate and drank with him after he rose from the dead. *(Acts 10:39-41)*

Cruciform–When Christ who is your life is revealed, then you also will be revealed with him in glory. *(Galatians 3:4)*

Week–Do not be afraid; I know that you are looking for Jesus who was crucified. He is not here; for he has been raised. *(Matthew 28:5)*

Closing–O God, who for our redemption gave your only-begotten Son to the death of the cross, and by his glorious resurrection delivered us from the power of our enemy: Grant us so to die daily to sin, that we may evermore live with him in the joy of his resurrection; through Jesus Christ your Son our Lord, who lives and reigns with you and the Holy Spirit, one God, now and for ever. Amen. *(BCP)*

Cross–Alleluia. The Lord is risen indeed: Come, let us adore him. Alleluia. *(BCP)*

Invitatory–When it was evening on that day, the first day of the week, and the doors of the house where the disciples had met were locked for fear of the Jews, Jesus came and stood among them and said, "Peace be with you." *(John 20:19)*

Cruciform–You will show me the path of life; in your presence there is fullness of joy, and in your right hand are pleasures for evermore. *(Psalm 16:11)*

Week–This Jesus God raised up, and of that all of us are witnesses. *(Acts 2:32)*

Closing–Almighty and everlasting God, who in the Paschal mystery established the new covenant of reconciliation: Grant that all who have been reborn into the fellowship of Christ's Body may show forth in their lives what they profess by their faith; through Jesus Christ our Lord, who lives and reigns with you and the Holy Spirit, one God, for ever and ever. Amen. *(BCP)*

Cross–Alleluia. The Lord is risen indeed: Come, let us adore him. Alleluia. *(BCP)*

Invitatory–O Lord, I am your servant; I am your servant and the child of your handmaid; you have freed me from my bonds. *(Psalm 116:16)*

Cruciform–Then their eyes were opened, and they recognized him; and he vanished from their sight. *(Luke 24:31)*

Week–Were not our hearts burning within us? *(Luke 24:32)*

Closing–O God, whose blessed Son made himself known to his disciples in the breaking of bread: Open the eyes of our faith, that we may behold him in all his redeeming work; who lives and reigns with you, in the unity of the Holy Spirit, one God, now and for ever. Amen. *(BCP)*

Cross–Alleluia. The Lord is risen indeed: Come, let us adore him. Alleluia. *(BCP)*

Invitatory–Those who had been baptized devoted themselves to the apostles' teaching and fellowship, to the breaking of bread and the prayers. *(Acts 2:42)*

Cruciform–Awe came upon everyone, because many wonders and signs were being done by the apostles. *(Acts 2:43)*

Week–I came that they may have life, and have it abundantly. *(John 10:10)*

Closing–O God, whose Son Jesus is the good shepherd of your people; Grant that when we hear his voice we may know him who calls us each by name, and follow where he leads; who, with you and the Holy Spirit, lives and reigns, one God, for ever and ever. Amen. *(BCP)*

Cross—Alleluia. The Lord is risen indeed: Come, let us adore him. Alleluia. *(BCP)*

Invitatory—In you, O Lord, have I taken refuge; let me never be put to shame; deliver me in your righteousness. *(Psalm 31:1)*

Cruciform—The stone that the builders rejected has become the very head of the corner. *(I Peter 2:7)*

Week—Lord Jesus, receive my spirit. *(Acts 7:59)*

Closing—Almighty God, whom truly to know is everlasting life: Grant us so perfectly to know your Son Jesus Christ to be the way, the truth, and the life, that we may steadfastly follow his steps in the way that leads to eternal life; through Jesus Christ your Son our Lord, who lives and reigns with you, in the unity of the Holy Spirit, one God, for ever and ever. Amen. *(BCP)*

Cross–Alleluia. The Lord is risen indeed: Come, let us adore him. Alleluia. *(BCP)*

Invitatory–For Christ also suffered for sins once for all, the righteous for the unrighteous, in order to bring you to God. *(I Peter 3:18)*

Cruciform–Those who love me will be loved by my Father, and I will love them and reveal myself to them. *(John 14:21)*

Week–In him we live and move and have our being. *(Acts 17:28)*

Closing–O God, you have prepared for those who love you such good things as surpass our understanding: Pour into our hearts such love towards you, that we, loving you in all things and above all things, may obtain your promises, which exceed all that we can desire; through Jesus Christ our Lord, who lives and reigns with you and the Holy Spirit, one God, for ever and ever. Amen. *(BCP)*

THE SEVENTH SUNDAY OF EASTER

Cross–Alleluia. The Lord is risen indeed: Come, let us adore him. Alleluia. *(BCP)*

Invitatory–When he had said this, as they were watching, he was lifted up, and a cloud took him out of their sight. *(Acts 1:9)*

Cruciform–Jesus looked up to heaven and said, "Father, the hour has come; glorify your Son. *(John 17:1)*

Week–Humble yourselves therefore under the mighty hand of God. *(I Peter 5:6)*

Closing–O God, the King of glory, you have exalted your only Son Jesus Christ with great triumph to your kingdom in heaven: Do not leave us comfortless, but send us your Holy Spirit to strengthen us, and exalt us to that place where our Savior Christ has gone before; who lives and reigns with you and the Holy Spirit, one God, in glory everlasting. Amen. *(BCP)*

Cross–Alleluia. The Spirit of the Lord renews the face of the earth: Come let us adore him. Alleluia. *(BCP)*

Invitatory–When he had said this, he breathed on them and said to them, "Receive the Holy Spirit. If you forgive the sins of any, they are forgiven them; if you retain the sins of any, they are retained." *(John 20:22)*

Cruciform–In those days I will pour out my Spirit; and they shall prophesy. *(Acts 2:17)*

Week–You send forth your Spirit, and they are created; and so you renew the face of the earth. *(Psalm 104:30)*

Closing–Almighty God, on this day you opened the way of eternal life to every race and nation by the promised gift of your Holy Spirit: Shed abroad this gift throughout the world by the preaching of the Gospel, that it may reach to the ends of the earth; through Jesus Christ our Lord, who lives and reigns with you, in the unity of the Holy Spirit, one God, for ever and ever. Amen. *(BCP)*

TRINITY SUNDAY

Cross–Father, Son, and Holy Spirit, one God: Come let us adore him. *(BCP)*

Invitatory–Then God said, "Let us make humankind in our image, according to our likeness; and let them have dominion. *(Genesis 1:26)*

Cruciform–The grace of the Lord Jesus Christ, the love of God, and the communion of the Holy Spirit be with all of you. *(2 Corinthians 13:14)*

Week–Go therefore and make disciples of all nations, baptizing them in the name of the Father and of the Son and of the Holy Spirit. *(Matthew 28:19)*

Closing–Almighty and everlasting God, you have given to us your servants grace, by the confession of a true faith, to acknowledge the glory of the eternal Trinity, and in the power of your divine Majesty to worship the Unity: Keep us steadfast in this faith and worship, and bring us at last to see you in your one and eternal glory, O Father; who with the Son and the Holy Spirit live and reign, one God, for ever and ever. Amen. *(BCP)*

PROPER 1
Week of the Sunday closest to May 11

Cross–The earth is the Lord's for he made it: Come let us adore him. (BCP)

Invitatory–Choose life so that you and your descendants may live, loving the Lord your God, obeying him, and holding fast to him. *(Deuteronomy 30:20)*

Cruciform–You laid down your commandments, that we should fully keep them. *(Psalm 199:4)*

Week–For we are God's servants, working together; you are God's field, God's building. *(I Corinthians 3:9)*

Closing–O God, the strength of all who put their trust in you: Mercifully accept our prayers; and because in our weakness we can do nothing good without you, give us the help of your grace, that in keeping your commandments we may please you both in will and deed; through Jesus Christ our Lord, who lives and reigns with you and the Holy Spirit, one God, for ever and ever. Amen. *(BCP)*

PROPER 2
Week of the Sunday closest to May 18

Cross—Worship the Lord in the beauty of holiness: Come let us adore him. (BCP)

Invitatory—But I say to you, Love your enemies and pray for those who persecute you, so that you may be children of your Father in heaven. *(Matthew 5:44-45)*

Cruciform—Do you not know that you are God's temple and that God's Spirit dwells in you? *(I Corinthians 3:16)*

Week—All belong to you, and you belong to Christ, and Christ belongs to God. *(I Corinthians 3:23)*

Closing—O Lord, you have taught us that without love whatever we do is worth nothing; Send your Holy Spirit and pour into our hearts your greatest gift, which is love, the true bond of peace and of all virtue, without which whoever lives is accounted dead before you. Grant this for the sake of your only Son Jesus Christ, who lives and reigns with you and the Holy Spirit, one God, now and for ever. Amen. *(BCP)*

Cross–The mercy of the Lord is everlasting: Come let us adore him. (BCP)

Invitatory–Therefore I tell you, do not worry about your life, what you will eat or what you will drink, or about your body, what you will wear. Is not life more than food, and the body more than clothing? *(Matthew 6:25)*

Cruciform–Look at the birds of the air; they neither sow nor reap nor gather into barns, and yet your heavenly Father feeds them. *(Matthew 6:26)*

Week–Strive for the kingdom of God and his righteousness, and all these things will be given to you as well. *(Matthew 6:33)*

Closing–Most loving Father, whose will it is for us to give thanks for all things, to fear nothing but the loss of you, and to cast all our care on you who care for us: Preserve us from faithless fears and worldly anxieties, that no clouds of this mortal life may hide from us the light of that love which is immortal, and which you have manifested to us in your Son Jesus Christ our Lord; who lives and reigns with you, in the unity of the Holy Spirit, one God, now and for ever. Amen. *(BCP)*

PROPER 4
Week of the Sunday closest to June 1

Cross—The earth is the Lord's for he made it: Come let us adore him. *(BCP)*

Invitatory—For I am not ashamed of the gospel; it is the power of God for salvation to everyone who has faith. *(Romans 1:16)*

Cruciform—Everyone who hears these words of mine and acts on them will be like a wise man who built his house on rock. *(Matthew 7:24)*

Week—You shall put these words of mine in your heart and soul. *(Deuteronomy 11:18)*

Closing—O God, your never-failing providence sets in order all things both in heaven and earth: Put away from us, we entreat you, all hurtful things, and give us those things which are profitable for us; through Jesus Christ our Lord, who lives and reigns with you and the Holy Spirit, one God, for ever and ever. Amen. *(BCP)*

PROPER 5
Week of the Sunday closest to June 8

Cross–Worship the Lord in the beauty of holiness: Come let us adore him. *(BCP)*

Invitatory–I desire mercy, not sacrifice. For I have come to call not the righteous but sinners. *(Matthew 9:13)*

Cruciform–Let us press on to know the Lord; his appearing is as sure as the dawn. *(Hosea 6:3)*

Week–For this reason it depends on faith, in order that the promise may rest on grace. *(Romans 4:16)*

Closing–O God, from whom all good proceeds: Grant that by your inspiration we may think those things that are right, and by your merciful guiding may do them; through Jesus Christ our Lord, who lives and reigns with you and the Holy Spirit, one God, for ever and ever. Amen. *(BCP)*

PROPER 6
Week of the Sunday closest to June 15

Cross–The mercy of the Lord is everlasting: Come let us adore him. *(BCP)*

Invitatory–Since we are justified by faith, we have peace with God through our Lord Jesus Christ, through whom we have obtained access to this grace in which we stand. *(Romans 5:1)*

Cruciform–As you go, proclaim the good news, 'The kingdom of heaven has come near.' *(Matthew 10:7)*

Week–The Lord is good; his mercy is everlasting; and his faithfulness endures from age to age. *(Psalm 100:5)*

Closing–Keep, O Lord, your household the Church in your steadfast faith and love, that through your grace we may proclaim your truth with boldness, and minister your justice with compassion; for the sake of our Savior Jesus Christ, who lives and reigns with you and the Holy Spirit, one God, now and for ever. Amen. *(BCP)*

PROPER 7
Week of the Sunday closest to June 22

Cross—The earth is the Lord's, for he made it: Come let us adore him. *(BCP)*

Invitatory—We know that Christ, being raised from the dead, will never die again; death no longer has dominion over him. *(Romans 6:9)*

Cruciform—Answer me, O Lord, for your love is kind; in your great compassion, turn to me.' *(Psalm 69:16)*

Week—Those who find their life will lose it, and those who lose their life for my sake will find it. *(Matthew 10:39)*

Closing—O Lord, make us have perpetual love and reverence for your holy Name, for you never fail to help and govern those whom you have set upon the sure foundation of your loving-kindness; through Jesus Christ our Lord, who lives and reigns with you and the Holy Spirit, one God, for ever and ever. Amen. *(BCP)*

PROPER 8

Week of the Sunday closest to June 29

Cross—Worship the Lord in the beauty of holiness: Come let us adore him. *(BCP)*

Invitatory—Whoever welcomes you welcomes me, and whoever welcomes me welcomes the one who sent me. *(Matthew 10:40)*

Cruciform—For the wages of sin is death, but the free gift of God is eternal life in Christ Jesus our Lord. *(Romans 6:23)*

Week—Your love, O Lord, for ever will I sing; from age to age my mouth will proclaim your faithfulness. *(Psalm 89:1)*

Closing—Almighty God, you have built your Church upon the foundation of the apostles and prophets, Jesus Christ himself being the chief cornerstone: Grant us so to be joined together in unity of spirit by their teaching, that we may be made a holy temple acceptable to you; through Jesus Christ our Lord, who lives and reigns with you and the Holy Spirit, one God, for ever and ever. Amen. *(BCP)*

Week of the Sunday closest to July 6

Cross–The mercy of the Lord is everlasting: Come let us adore him. *(BCP)*

Invitatory–Come to me, all you that are weary and are carrying heavy burdens, and I will give you rest. *(Matthew 11:28)*

Cruciform–Take my yoke upon you, and learn from me; for I am gentle and humble in heart, and you will find rest for your souls. *(Matthew 11:29)*

Week–For my yoke is easy, and my burden is light. *(Matthew 11:30)*

Closing–O God, you have taught us to keep all your commandments by loving you and our neighbor: Grant us the grace of your Holy Spirit, that we may be devoted to you with our whole heart, and united to one another with pure affection; through Jesus Christ our Lord, who lives and reigns with you and the Holy Spirit, one God, for ever and ever. Amen. *(BCP)*

PROPER 10
Week of the Sunday closest to July 23

Cross—The earth is the Lord's, for he made it: Come let us adore him. *(BCP)*

Invitatory—As for what was sown on good soil, this is the one who hears the word and understands it, who indeed bears fruit. *(Matthew 13:23)*

Cruciform—You are not in the flesh; you are in the Spirit, since the Spirit of God dwells in you. *(Romans 8:9)*

Week—You shall go out in joy, and be led back in peace. *(Isaiah 55:12)*

Closing—O Lord, mercifully receive the prayers of your people who call upon you, and grant that they may know and understand what things they ought to do, and also may have grace and power faithfully to accomplish them; through Jesus Christ our Lord, who lives and reigns with you and the Holy Spirit, one God, now and for ever. Amen. *(BCP)*

PROPER 11
Week of the Sunday closest to July 20

Cross–Worship the Lord in the beauty of holiness: Come let us adore him. *(BCP)*

Invitatory–When we cry, "Abba! Father!" it is that very Spirit bearing witness with our spirit that we are children of God. *(Romans 8:16)*

Cruciform–The righteous will shine like the sun in the kingdom of their Father. *(Matthew 13:43)*

Week–Do not fear, or be afraid; have I not told you from of old and declared it? *(Isaiah 44:8)*

Closing–Almighty God, the fountain of all wisdom, you know our necessities before we ask and our ignorance in asking: Have compassion on our weakness, and mercifully give us those things which for our unworthiness we dare not, and for our blindness we cannot ask; through the worthiness of your Son Jesus Christ our Lord, who lives and reigns with you and the Holy Spirit, one God, now and for ever. Amen. *(BCP)*

Week of the Sunday closest to July 27

Cross–The mercy of the Lord is everlasting: Come let us adore him. *(BCP)*

Invitatory–The kingdom of heaven is like a mustard seed that someone took and sowed in his field; it is the smallest of all the seeds, but when it has grown it is the greatest of shrubs. *(Matthew 13:32)*

Cruciform–The Spirit helps us in our weakness; for we do not know how to pray as we ought, but that very Spirit intercedes with sighs too deep for words. *(Romans 8:26)*

Week–Your decrees are wonderful; therefore I obey them with all my heart. *(Psalm 119:129)*

Closing–O God, the protector of all who trust in you, without whom nothing is strong, nothing is holy: Increase and multiply upon us your mercy; that, with you as our ruler and guide, we may so pass through things temporal, that we lose not the things eternal; through Jesus Christ our Lord, who lives and reigns with you and the Holy Spirit, one God, for ever and ever. Amen. *(BCP)*

PROPER 13
Week of the Sunday closest to August 3

Cross—The earth is the Lord's, for he made it: Come let us adore him. *(BCP)*

Invitatory—Jesus ordered the crowds to sit down on the grass. Taking the five loaves and the two fish, he looked up to heaven, and blessed and broke the loaves, and gave them to the disciples, and the disciples gave them to the crowds. And all ate and were filled. *(Matthew 14:19)*

Cruciform—The Lord is gracious and full of compassion, slow to anger and of great kindness. *(Psalm 145:8)*

Week—Ho, everyone who thirsts, come to the waters. *(Isaiah 55:1)*

Closing—Let your continual mercy, O Lord, cleanse and defend your Church; and, because it cannot continue in safety without your help, protect and govern it always by your goodness; through Jesus Christ our Lord, who lives and reigns with you and the Holy Spirit, one God, for ever and ever. Amen. *(BCP)*

PROPER 14
Week of the Sunday closest to August 10

Cross—Worship the Lord in the beauty of holiness: Come let us adore him. *(BCP)*

Invitatory—I will listen to what the Lord God is saying, for he is speaking peace to his faithful people and to those who turn their hearts to him. *(Psalm 85:8)*

Cruciform—Everyone who calls on the name of the Lord shall be saved. *(Romans 10:13)*

Week—Take heart, it is I; do not be afraid. *(Matthew 14:27)*

Closing—Grant to us, Lord, we pray, the spirit to think and do always those things that are right, that we, who cannot exist without you, may by you be enabled to live according to your will; through Jesus Christ our Lord, who lives and reigns with you and the Holy Spirit, one God, for ever and ever. Amen. *(BCP)*

PROPER 15

Week of the Sunday closest to August 17

Cross—The mercy of the Lord is everlasting: Come let us adore him. *(BCP)*

Invitatory—For my house shall be called a house of prayer for all peoples. *(Isaiah 56:7)*

Cruciform—For the gifts and the calling of God are irrevocable. *(Romans 11:29)*

Week—Have mercy on me, Lord, Son of David. *(Matthew 15:22)*

Closing—Almighty God, you have given your only Son to be for us a sacrifice for sin, and also an example of godly life: Give us grace to receive thankfully the fruits of his redeeming work, and to follow daily in the blessed steps of his most holy life; through Jesus Christ your Son our Lord, who lives and reigns with you and the Holy Spirit, one God, now and for ever. Amen. *(BCP)*

PROPER 16
Week of the Sunday closest to August 24

Cross—The earth is the Lord's, for he made it: Come let us adore him. *(BCP)*

Invitatory—Lift up your eyes to the heavens, and look at the earth beneath; my salvation will be for ever, and my deliverance will never be ended. *(Isaiah 51:6)*

Cruciform—Do not be conformed to this world, but be transformed by the renewing of your minds. *(Romans 12:2)*

Week—You are the Messiah, the Son of the living God. *(Matthew 16:16)*

Closing—Grant, O merciful God, that your Church, being gathered together in unity by your Holy Spirit, may show forth your power among all peoples, to the glory of your Name; through Jesus Christ our Lord, who lives and reigns with you and the Holy Spirit, one God, for ever and ever. Amen. *(BCP)*

PROPER 17

Cross–Worship the Lord in the beauty of holiness: Come let us adore him. *(BCP)*

Invitatory–If any want to become my followers, let them deny themselves and take up their cross and follow me. *(Matthew 16:24)*

Cruciform–For those who want to save their life will lose it, and those who lose their life for my sake will find it. *(Matthew 16:25)*

Week–For the Son of Man is to come with his angels in the glory of his Father. *(Matthew 16:27)*

Closing–Lord of all power and might, the author and giver of all good things: Graft in our hearts the love of your Name; increase in us true religion; nourish us with all goodness; and bring forth in us the fruit of good works; through Jesus Christ our Lord, who lives and reigns with you and the Holy Spirit, one God, for ever and ever. Amen. *(BCP)*

Cross—The mercy of the Lord is everlasting: Come let us adore him. *(BCP)*

Invitatory—Truly I tell you, whatever you bind on earth will be bound in heaven, and whatever you loose on earth will be loosed in heaven. *(Matthew 18:18)*

Cruciform—Again, truly I tell you, if two of you agree on earth about anything you ask, it will be done for you by my Father in heaven. *(Matthew 18:19)*

Week—For where two or three are gathered in my name, I am there among them. *(Matthew 18:20)*

Closing—Grant us, O Lord, to trust in you with all our hearts; for, as you always resist the proud who confide in their own strength, so you never forsake those who make their boast of your mercy; through Jesus Christ our Lord, who lives and reigns with you and the Holy Spirit, one God, now and for ever. Amen. *(BCP)*

PROPER 19

Week of the Sunday closest to September 14

Cross—The earth is the Lord's, for he made it: Come let us adore him. *(BCP)*

Invitatory—We do not live to ourselves, and we do not die to ourselves. If we live, we live to the Lord, and if we die, we die to the Lord; so then, whether we live or whether we die, we are the Lord's. *(Romans 14:7)*

Cruciform—For to this end Christ died and lived again, so that he might be Lord of both the dead and the living. *(Romans 14:9)*

Week—Bless the Lord, O my soul, and all that is within me, bless his holy Name. *(Psalm 103:1)*

Closing—O God, because without you we are not able to please you, mercifully grant that your Holy Spirit may in all things direct and rule our hearts; through Jesus Christ our Lord, who lives and reigns with you and the Holy Spirit, one God, now and for ever. Amen. *(BCP)*

PROPER 20

Week of the Sunday closest to September 21

Cross—Worship the Lord in the beauty of holiness: Come let us adore him. *(BCP)*

Invitatory—Only, live your life in a manner worthy of the gospel of Christ, so that, whether I come and see you or am absent and hear about you, I will know that you are standing firm in one spirit. *(Philippians 1:27)*

Cruciform—The Lord is gracious and full of compassion,
slow to anger and of great kindness. *(Psalm 145:8)*

Week—So the last will be first, and the first will be last. *(Matthew 20:16)*

Closing—Grant us, Lord, not to be anxious about earthly things, but to love things heavenly; and even now, while we are placed among things that are passing away, to hold fast to those that shall endure; through Jesus Christ our Lord, who lives and reigns with you and the Holy Spirit, one God, for ever and ever. Amen. *(BCP)*

PROPER 21

Week of the Sunday closest to September 28

Cross–The mercy of the Lord is everlasting: Come let us adore him. *(BCP)*

Invitatory–Do nothing from selfish ambition or conceit, but in humility regard others as better than yourselves. *(Philippians 2:3)*

Cruciform–Let each of you look not to your own interests, but to the interests of others. *(Philippians 2:4)*

Week–Let the same mind be in you that was in Christ Jesus. *(Philippians 2:5)*

Closing–O God, you declare your almighty power chiefly in showing mercy and pity: Grant us the fullness of your grace, that we, running to obtain your promises, may become partakers of your heavenly treasure; through Jesus Christ our Lord, who lives and reigns with you and the Holy Spirit, one God, for ever and ever. Amen. *(BCP)*

PROPER 22

Week of the Sunday closest to October 5

Cross–The earth is the Lord's, for he made it: Come let us adore him. *(BCP)*

Invitatory–The stone that the builders rejected has become the cornerstone; this was the Lord's doing, and it is amazing in our eyes. *(Matthew 21:42)*

Cruciform–Forgetting what lies behind and straining forward to what lies ahead, I press on toward the goal for the prize of the heavenly call of God in Christ Jesus. *(Philippians 3:13-14)*

Week–Restore us, O God of hosts; show the light of your countenance, and we shall be saved. *(Psalm 80:18)*

Closing–Almighty and everlasting God, you are always more ready to hear than we to pray, and to give more than we either desire or deserve: Pour upon us the abundance of your mercy, forgiving us those things of which our conscience is afraid, and giving us those good things for which we are not worthy to ask, except through the merits and mediation of Jesus Christ our Savior; who lives and reigns with you and the Holy Spirit, one God, for ever and ever. Amen. *(BCP)*

Cross—Worship the Lord in the beauty of holiness: Come let us adore him. *(BCP)*

Invitatory—Rejoice in the Lord always; again I will say, Rejoice. Let your gentleness be known to everyone. The Lord is near. *(Philippians 4:4)*

Cruciform—Do not worry about anything, but in everything by prayer and supplication with thanksgiving let your requests be made known to God. *(Philippians 4:6)*

Week—The peace of God, which surpasses all understanding, will guard your hearts and your minds in Christ Jesus. *(Philippians 4:7)*

Closing—Lord, we pray that your grace may always precede and follow us, that we may continually be given to good works; through Jesus Christ our Lord, who lives and reigns with you and the Holy Spirit, one God, now and for ever. Amen. *(BCP)*

Week of the Sunday closest to October 19

Cross–The mercy of the Lord is everlasting: Come let us adore him. *(BCP)*

Invitatory–For we know, brothers and sisters beloved by God, that he has chosen you, because our message of the gospel came to you not in word only, but also in power and in the Holy Spirit and with full conviction. *(1 Thessalonians 1:4-5)*

Cruciform–Give therefore to the emperor the things that are the emperor's, and to God the things that are God's. *(Matthew 22:21)*

Week–Ascribe to the Lord the honor due his Name; bring offerings and come into his courts. *(Psalm 96:8)*

Closing–Almighty and everlasting God, in Christ you have revealed your glory among the nations: Preserve the works of your mercy, that your Church throughout the world may persevere with steadfast faith in the confession of your Name; through Jesus Christ our Lord, who lives and reigns with you and the Holy Spirit, one God, for ever and ever. Amen. *(BCP)*

Cross—The earth is the Lord's, for he made it: Come let us adore him. *(BCP)*

Invitatory—For our appeal does not spring from deceit or impure motives or trickery, but just as we have been approved by God to be entrusted with the message of the gospel, even so we speak, not to please mortals, but to please God who tests our hearts. (*1 Thessalonians 2:3-4*)

Cruciform—You shall love the Lord your God with all your heart, and with all your soul, and with all your mind.' This is the greatest and first commandment. And a second is like it: 'You shall love your neighbor as yourself.' *(Matthew 22:37)*

Week—You shall be holy, for I the Lord your God am holy. (*Leviticus 19:2*)

Closing—Almighty and everlasting God, increase in us the gifts of faith, hope, and charity; and, that we may obtain what you promise, make us love what you command; through Jesus Christ our Lord, who lives and reigns with you and the Holy Spirit, one God, for ever and ever. Amen. *(BCP)*

PROPER 26
Week of the Sunday closest to November 2

Cross–Worship the Lord in the beauty of holiness: Come let us adore him. *(BCP)*

Invitatory–When you received the word of God that you heard from us, you accepted it not as a human word but as what it really is, God's word, which is also at work in you believers. (*1 Thessalonians 2:13*)

Cruciform–Send out your light and your truth, that they may lead me, and bring me to your holy hill and to your dwelling. (*Psalm 43:3*)

Week–All who exalt themselves will be humbled, and all who humble themselves will be exalted. (*Matthew 23:12*)

Closing–Almighty and merciful God, it is only by your gift that your faithful people offer you true and laudable service: Grant that we may run without stumbling to obtain your heavenly promises; through Jesus Christ our Lord, who lives and reigns with you and the Holy Spirit, one God, now and for ever. Amen. *(BCP)*

PROPER 27

Week of the Sunday closest to November 9

Cross–The mercy of the Lord is everlasting: Come let us adore him. *(BCP)*

Invitatory–The Lord himself, with a cry of command, with the archangel's call and with the sound of God's trumpet, will descend from heaven, and the dead in Christ will rise first. *(1 Thessalonians 4:16)*

Cruciform–You are my helper and my deliverer; O Lord, do not tarry. *(Psalm 70:6)*

Week–Keep awake therefore, for you know neither the day nor the hour. *(Matthew 25:13)*

Closing–O God, whose blessed Son came into the world that he might destroy the works of the devil and make us children of God and heirs of eternal life: Grant that, having this hope, we may purify ourselves as he is pure; that, when he comes again with power and great glory, we may be made like him in his eternal and glorious kingdom; where he lives and reigns with you and the Holy Spirit, one God, for ever and ever. Amen. *(BCP)*

PROPER 28

Week of the Sunday closest to November 16

Cross—The earth is the Lord's, for he made it: Come let us adore him. *(BCP)*

Invitatory—For you yourselves know very well that the day of the Lord will come like a thief in the night. *(1 Thessalonians 5:2)*

Cruciform—So then let us not fall asleep as others do, but let us keep awake and be sober. *(1 Thessalonians 5:6)*

Week—Since we belong to the day, let us be sober, and put on the breastplate of faith and love, and for a helmet the hope of salvation. *(1 Thessalonians 5:6)*

Closing—Blessed Lord, who caused all holy Scriptures to be written for our learning: Grant us so to hear them, read, mark, learn, and inwardly digest them, that we may embrace and ever hold fast the blessed hope of everlasting life, which you have given us in our Savior Jesus Christ; who lives and reigns with you and the Holy Spirit, one God, for ever and ever. Amen. *(BCP)*

PROPER 29
Week of the Sunday closest to November 23

Cross—Worship the Lord in the beauty of holiness: Come let us adore him. *(BCP)*

Invitatory—Come, you that are blessed by my Father, inherit the kingdom prepared for you from the foundation of the world. *(Matthew 25:34)*

Cruciform—I was hungry and you gave me food, I was thirsty and you gave me something to drink, I was a stranger and you welcomed me, I was naked and you gave me clothing, I was sick and you took care of me, I was in prison and you visited me. *(Matthew 25:35)*

Week—Truly I tell you, just as you did it to one of the least of these who are members of my family, you did it to me. *(Matthew 25:40)*

Closing—Almighty and everlasting God, whose will it is to restore all things in your well-beloved Son, the King of kings and Lord of lords: Mercifully grant that the peoples of the earth, divided and enslaved by sin, may be freed and brought together under his most gracious rule; who lives and reigns with you and the Holy Spirit, one God, now and for ever. Amen. *(BCP)*